PRAISE FOR *THE SAGE'S TAO TE CHING*

"Here is wisdom that is beauty and beauty that is wisdom. William Martin's final book of his *Tao Te Ching* trilogy is a masterpiece. It illuminates all the unexplored potentials inherent in the second half of life and eases the mind into each one. Powerful, lyrical, insightful, *The Sage's Tao Te Ching* is a guide that will lead your heart gently and surely to 'life itself.'"

—HUGH AND GAYLE PRATHER, authors of
The Little Book of Letting Go

"Let this gem of a book and the wisdom it imparts enfold every aspect of your being. Whatever time you have remaining on this planet will be immensely enriched."

—DAVID MCNALLY, author of
Even Eagles Need a Push

"Like its predecessors, *The Sage's Tao Te Ching* opens our minds to the wisdom of our natural state and encourages us to accept and honor the inevitability of the wonder-filled grace of aging. Bill Martin deserves our humble gratitude for reacquainting us with our true selves."

—from the foreword by
CHUNGLIANG AL HUANG

THE EXPERIMENT

BECAUSE EVERY BOOK IS A TEST OF NEW IDEAS

TENTH ANNIVERSARY EDITION

■

THE SAGE'S TAO TE CHING

■

ANCIENT ADVICE
FOR
THE SECOND HALF OF LIFE

■

WILLIAM MARTIN

FOREWORD BY CHUNGLIANG AL HUANG
ILLUSTRATIONS BY HANK TUSINSKI

THE EXPERIMENT
NEW YORK

THE SAGE'S TAO TE CHING:
ANCIENT ADVICE FOR THE SECOND HALF OF LIFE—
TENTH ANNIVERSARY EDITION
Copyright © William Martin 2000, 2010
Foreword copyright © Chungliang Al Huang 2000
Illustrations copyright © Hank Tusinski 2000

The Experiment, LLC
220 East 23rd Street, Suite 600
New York, NY 10010-6458
theexperimentpublishing.com

Library of Congress Control Number: 2010924703

ISBN: 978-1-61519-024-9
Ebook ISBN: 978-1-61519-128-4

Cover design by Nita Ybarra
Cover photograph by Lonny Kalfus | Getty Images
Design by Pauline Neuwirth, Neuwirth & Associates, Inc.

Manufactured in the United States

Tenth anniversary edition first published August 2010

15 14 13 12 11 10 9 8

To George Fowler, who returned to the Tao ten years ago.

George, you showed me what a true sage looks like.

May your dance eternally endure.

CONTENTS

■

■

MORE THAN TWO thousand five hundred years ago, when Confucius reached the venerable age of seventy, he took the occasion to reflect on his life: "At fifteen I was committed to learning. At thirty I took my rightful position. At forty, I was no longer totally perplexed. At fifty, I began to understand the unfolding of my true nature. At sixty, I was in harmony with contradictions and ambivalence. At seventy, at long last, I may follow my heart's desire without going astray." Even for this master sage, becoming wise required a lifetime of work.

Confucius and his disciples produced reams of writing in a conscientious effort to enlighten the masses. In contrast, Lao Tzu, who according to legend was Confucius' contemporary and teacher, wrote five thousand words, most of those in his *Tao Te Ching*. Several hundred generations later, those eighty-one poetic verses continue to inspire seekers of truth and wisdom and translators in languages spoken everywhere on the globe.

Twelve years ago William Martin embarked on an ingenious and novel enterprise—mining and crystallizing the essential teachings of the *Tao Te Ching* for specific audiences. He addressed his first volume to parents, his second to loving couples. As difficult and foolhardy as it may be to set out to improve on a classic, William Martin has arguably done just that. While he has remained faithful to the spirit of the *Tao Te Ching*, his words maintain all the original wisdom of Lao Tzu's, yet identify themes and situations that resonate especially with parents and couples.

Now you hold his third reinterpretation of the Tao in your hands. In his introduction Bill Martin tells us that the writing of this newest book coincides with his own "saging." Although those of us approaching or already in the midst of this saging third of our lives have much to appreciate and enjoy, the wisdom accumulated over a lifetime often clashes with the admonitions of others to pursue the life of the forever young. Each of us must come to terms with those messages that are at odds with who we have become. Like its predecessors, *The Sage's Tao Te Ching* helps us to do just that, opening our minds to the wisdom of our natural state and encouraging us to accept and honor the inevitability of the wonder-filled grace of aging. Bill Martin deserves our humble gratitude for reacquainting us with our true selves.

—CHUNGLIANG AL HUANG, founder and president of the Living Tao Foundation and author of *Embrace Tiger, Return to Mountain*

 I WROTE THIS interpretation of Lao Tzu's classic work of practical phi-losophy, the *Tao Te Ching*, when I was fifty-five years old. Now, ten years later, as it is being reissued in a tenth anniversary edition, I am delighted to have the opportunity to revisit the introduction and note, with heartfelt aware-ness, that it was much easier to write the words than it has been to live them these past ten years. Despite that awareness, I haven't altered my conviction that Lao Tzu's image of the "sage" is an essential model for a modern journey into wisdom. In fact, I am increasingly aware that, without a reemergence of the sage as the model for older people, we're in ever-greater danger of trivializing ourselves into further decay and decline.

In some respects, the terrorist attacks of September 11, 2001 appear to have driven us further into distraction and away from thoughtful consideration. We've turned not to wisdom but rather to fear and political polarization. Instead of heeding the courageous voices of our sages offering a path of compassion, we have turned to the voices that urge us to remain in our habitual patterns of consumption and distraction. I find myself deeply concerned as I watch so many older people sink into withdrawal and fear, casting about for ways to protect and isolate themselves.

Yet once again the voice of Lao Tzu reminds me that nothing has really changed over the past 2,500 years. Human beings have always been conditioned to look for easy and painless paths through difficulties. We don't want to face the sometimes painful path of compassion, empathy, and openness to the needs of other people. We naturally turn aside from discomfort and seek to reassure ourselves that we can ignore the needs of an interdependent world, a world deeply in need of healing and compassion. The guidance of Lao Tzu continues to offer an alternative. A deeper, more authentic way is always possible—for nations, for individuals, for me. The world continues to wait for word from the center of human wisdom. Who will speak this word if not those who have tried the other ways and found them inadequate, those who are finally willing and able to let go of useless desires and fears, to live and to say the truth with the force and compassion necessary for these times? Who will speak as sages to a world that needs their voice if not you and I?

The Sage's Tao Te Ching is my third interpreta-
tion of Lao Tzu. Like its predecessors, *The Parent's
Tao Te Ching* and *The Couple's Tao Te Ching*, it is an
expression of Taoist thought for our modern life.
The *Tao Te Ching* has been my guide through my
responsibilities and concerns as a parent and in
my relationship of love and intimacy with my
spouse—and over the past ten years it has been
my support in the latter part of my life, a period
when I have sought to live as a fearsome, powerful,
wonder-filled sage.

The sage in Chinese society has been a venerated
role for thousands of years. Indeed, it is assumed
that a person does not have the capacity for true
wisdom until the years have bestowed the benefits
arising from the full experience of such seeming
polarities as success and failure, gain and loss, love
and fear, sickness and health, and life and death.

Many traditional societies have venerated the
role of sage, but perhaps none more clearly than
the Chinese. The two formative philosophies of
Chinese history, Taoism and Confucianism, each
view the sage as the primary keeper and transmitter
of wisdom, culture, values, power, and spirituality.
For Lao Tzu, the principal voice of Taoism, the older
person who becomes a sage is a model of the life of
freedom and contentment to which all aspire. In his
Tao Te Ching, Lao Tzu writes eighty-one short poetic
chapters of advice which hold up the sage, sometimes called "master" or "wise one," as the essence of
humanity. In *The Sage's Tao Te Ching*, I have reformu-
lated what I believe to be the heart of each of Lao

Tzu's chapters into an insight or reflection for the older person in our particular modern society.

In the ten years since I wrote *The Sage's Tao Te Ching*, I have found that the actual process of becoming an elder keeper of wisdom and model of hope is far from easy. Merely growing ten years older has not automatically made me wise. I have struggled firsthand with the conditioned tendencies to restrict my perspective, tighten the reins on my life, and become self-protective and isolated. On the other hand, I have continued to live by the insights of Lao Tzu and to experience deep gratitude for the spaciousness, hope, serenity, and power they provide. I am facing the most important role of my life as I attempt to harvest my experience, gather my courage, access my wisdom, and prepare to live and to serve with the compassion and grace that is so greatly needed in my life and in my world.

Many of our societal structures have not supported me in my desire. On every side I have been reminded of our culture's idolization of youth. Advertisements portray senior citizens as healthy, wealthy, but not necessarily wise. We are urged to continue to be good consumers as we move into retirement communities, spending our carefully amassed pensions even as those pensions are decimated by the very systems that urge us to spend them.

A new model of aging is needed. Instead of attempting to be gray-haired teenagers still grasping at the illusory gusto of youth or, conversely, slipping into the depressive and curmudgeonly role of excess baggage, despairing of hope and waiting to die, we must recapture the traditional role of elder, or sage. Our society, more now than ten years ago, is desperate for a critical mass of older people to make this transformation. When they do, a revolution will occur that will help make the coming age not the Information Age, as we have been led to believe, but the Age of Wisdom.

The Sage's Tao Te Ching is, for me, the most satisfying of my interpretations of Lao Tzu's words. Growing older, coming to terms with my successes and failures, facing my own mortality, and watching my culture slip farther and farther into a "sound bite" understanding of life have brought me to the most crucial crossroads of my life. Will I be able to harvest my life in compassion and love for the world? Will I find in my own heart the wisdom for which I long? This question trumps all others for me. I suspect it is the same for you. We need each other more than ever. Around the world, small groups of elders are beginning to support one another as we engage in this monumental task. Our quest might just be the hero's journey of our time. I would enjoy sharing this journey with you in whatever way might be appropriate. I can be reached through The Still Point, the center in northern California where I am a teacher (www.thestillpoint.com).

May the power and wisdom inherent in the mysterious Tao surround us all.

BILL MARTIN
Chico, California
February 2010

THE SAGE'S
TAO TE CHING

■

OLDER OR WISER?

Growing older either reveals or hides
the mystery of existence.

If you are becoming a sage
you will grow in trust and contentment.
You will discover the light
of life's deepest truths.
If you are merely growing older,
you will become trapped by fears and frustrations.
You will see only the darkness
of infirmity and death.

The great task of the sage
is learning to see in the darkness
and not be afraid.

There is one primary choice
facing every aging person:
Will we become sages,
harvesting the spiritual essence of our lives
and blessing all future generations?
Or will we just grow older,
withdrawing,
circling the wagons,
and waiting for the end?

2

PUTTING IT ALL TOGETHER

Many in our culture
regard youth as good
and old age as bad.
But is this true?

In the sage, youth and age are married.
Wisdom and folly have each been lived fully.
Innocence and experience now support one
        another.
Action and rest follow each other easily.
Life and death have become inseparable.

The sage has experienced all opposites
and lets them come and go
without clinging or fretting.
Therefore the sage can talk without lecturing,
act without worrying about results,
and live in contentment with all events.

The first part of our life
was spent separating things into categories:
good and bad,
like and dislike,
me and you,
us and them.
Now it is time to put all the pieces back together
into a seamless whole.

3

EVERY ORDINARY MOMENT

We are learning to distinguish
between true and false power.
We see the clamoring of the young
for wealth and position
and we sadly smile and shake our heads.

We are less attached to our possessions
and no longer dominated by great ambition.
We are not enslaved by our desires
and therefore not as vulnerable to the schemes of
        others.

Our thoughts are becoming clearer,
and our needs are becoming more simple.
Enough to eat,
a comfortable bed,
and the glow of friendship
suffice to delight us.

Isn't it wonderful to have friends visit
and to talk of gentle, hopeful things?
How pleasant to enjoy the aroma of morning coffee
and a sip of sherry before bed.
We have earned the right
to enjoy every ordinary moment.

4

WE ARE OLDER
BUT NOT WITHERED

We are older
but not withered.
We are like the Tao,
always the source of new things.
The years can not harden
the suppleness of our soul,
nor dry the wellsprings of our heart.
Our flexible mind
keeps our body soft and loose.
We are like a newborn baby
in so many wonderful ways:
open, delighted,
curious and unafraid.

It may sometimes seem
that the juices are gone.
But they are not.
Do something every day that increases suppleness.
Listen to music you've never heard before.
Read a book by an unfamiliar author.
Practice simple yoga or Tai Chi for your body.
Walk in natural beauty.
Talk gently with a lonely person.
You will be surprised and delighted
at the river of compassion
that flows within you.

5

OUR HEART HAS EXPANDED WITH COMPASSION

As we grow in age
we grow also in acceptance.
We see shades of gray
instead of black and white.
We become slow to condemn
and quick to forgive.

We do not rant and rave.
We do not complain and gripe.
Our heart has expanded with compassion
and is open to all people.

Bitterness and cynicism abound
but you do not have to partake.
Think of an individual or organization
whose actions have upset you.
Write them a letter thanking them
for the benefits they provide
and encouraging them
in the difficult work they do.
Tell them you understand
how difficult it is
to satisfy everyone.
Notice how such an action
will make you feel.

6

We Cannot Exhaust the Tao

We are not dying,
merely changing.
We are a dance of atomic energy
that can never be destroyed,
only transformed.
Each breath we take is a rebirth.
Even our last breath
will bring something new.
We cannot exhaust
the energy of the Tao.

The physical atoms that make up your body
have been completely replaced
in the past nine years.
Yet you remain.
You may feel the effects of age,
but your spirit is always renewed
in each and every moment.
Remember this when you are tired or ill.
Let each breath renew your spirit.

7

We Are Free at Last

Growing older brings detachment
from temporary things.
But the more detached we become,
the more passionately we live.
We even become detached from ourselves,
and enjoy ourselves more than ever.

Like the Tao we have no desires for ourselves,
yet all our desires are fulfilled.
We have no more need for accomplishment
yet we accomplish everything.
We accept the fact of death
yet find we are always alive.

The detachment of the sage
is not a stoic withdrawal from life.
It is a delightful immersion
in every aspect of living.
But we no longer need to take ourselves
so terribly seriously.
We are free at last
to live with joy and love,
instead of fear and distrust.

8

WHAT HAVE WE BEEN PURSUING?

What have we been pursuing all our life?
Have we been looking for respect,
for financial security,
the approval of others,
or the comfort of a fine home?
Perhaps we wanted a family to love,
and a government to care for our needs?

Now we have discovered that
the only respect worth having
is self-respect.
The only security available
comes from serving other people.
The only approval we need is our own.
The simple home is happiest.
True love is compassion for all beings.
And the Tao alone meets all our needs.

Whatever your present circumstances,
a serene response is possible.
Whatever your health,
contentment is available.
Whatever your losses,
hope and happiness can be yours.
Act each day with compassion
for yourself and others.
Let each inhalation bring you peace
and each exhalation dispel your fears.

9

THE SAGE DOES NOT RETIRE
FROM LIFE

The sage does not retire from life.
The sage retires from unhappiness.

Images of silver-haired couples
strolling on golf courses
and basking on resort beaches
distort the idea of retirement.
Retirement is about doing
what we should always have been doing:
Living freely and happily
with joy and compassion for all.

You do not need to add to your IRA
for another five years
in order to retire.
Retire now!

Retire from worry.
Retire from the pursuit of possessions.
Retire from complaining.
Retire from the strain
of seeking security.
Retire from unhappiness.

Enjoy the moments given you.
Love the people around you.
Live the life offered you.

10

Training Mind, Body, and Heart

Many say that growing older causes
the mind to wander,
the body to stiffen,
and the heart to harden.

This is not the case for us.
As we become sages
our minds begin to see the oneness of all things,
our bodies become more flexible and supple,
and our hearts soften in love.

You can train your mind
through meditation, reading,
and mental exercise.
You can train your body
through yoga, Tai Chi,
and physical exercise.
You can train your heart
through listening, accepting,
and forgiving all.

11

WHAT HAS BEEN
COOKING WITHIN?

Memories and feelings over the years
have formed an "I" that seems so solid.
But just as the walls of a house form
a protected space where people live,
this "I" merely provides a platform
for the experience of life.

The body has a shape and a form
and seems so important.
But like a cooking pot,
it is the space inside that is important.
The body is a mere pot.
What has been cooking within
all these years?

The time has come to redefine ourselves.
We are not our memories,
important though they are.
We are not our bodies,
familiar though they are.
There is something else here,
mysterious and elusive.
What is it?

12

THERE IS ALWAYS ROOM FOR LIFE

Some older people despair
from having seen too much,
heard too much,
and felt too much.
The mind has become crowded
with sorrow and fear.
There is no more room
for hopes and dreams.

But the sage is always releasing things;
releasing thoughts,
releasing fears,
releasing expectations.
In the sage's mind there is always room for life.

Let your memories, good and bad,
come and go without lingering.
These are not you.
They are merely images
projected on the screen of your mind.
Don't be trapped in this dark theater.
Go outside and meet the life
set before you in this moment.

13

READY TO BE OF SERVICE

The sage is old enough now
to see through success and failure.
These illusions no longer dominate.

The sage has climbed up ladders,
climbed down ladders,
and fallen from ladders.
Now, with feet firmly on the ground,
the sage is ready to be of service to others,
not to get something from them,
but for the pure pleasure of it.

We have traded services for money all our life.
We have forgotten the joy of serving
simply because it is our nature.
As a sage we may still be paid for our services,
but it is no longer the determining factor.
When the opportunity for service arises
we no longer weigh the possible return.
We are free to serve
according to our nature.

14

FINDING NEW QUESTIONS

We have ceased trying
to tie up all loose ends.
We have discovered
that life does not need to be neat.
We have more questions than answers,
and this is a great delight to us.
We trust the Mystery of life
without having to possess It.
We cherish the feeling of awe
that has grown within our soul.

Some see answers as strong
and questions as weak.
Successful politicians have all the answers.
But I tell you the truth:
The happy person is not the one
with all the answers.
Each new question is an affirmation
of the delight of living.
What new question have you discovered today?

15

What Does a Sage Look Like?

What does a sage look like?
Moving with the grace of a deer
stepping through the meadow;
Alert to everything around,
never lost in the swamp of thoughts;
Always polite and generous,
never cynical or cranky;
Adaptable and flexible,
never rigid or stubborn;
Accepting of everyone,
rejecting no one.

Consider our caricatures of elders:
hazardous behind the wheel,
set in their ways,
impatient and intolerant.
Let us put these myths to rest.
Our driving is alert and mindful,
not aggressive, not hurried,
yet providing no obstruction to others.
We delight in learning new things.
And we are coming to accept all living beings
with compassion and grace.

16

DEATH IS OUR COMPANION

Death is the companion of every sage,
a friend who shares the path with us
and who provides a welcome
at our journey's end.

This friendship seems unnatural to many,
but it is a source of great wisdom.
Cultivating this friendship requires courage,
honesty, and openness.
We must visit the dark regions of our mind,
the places where our unnamed fears reside.
There we must wait until these fears dissolve.
Then we will return with a light
that will illumine the rest of our path.

Befriending death is not morbid.
It is not depressing.
It is not giving up on living.
It is merely accepting the natural boundary
given to life for our benefit.
It is up to you to shine a light
upon the path of life
so those who follow you
might walk without fear.

17

Encourage Their Dreams

Some do their work in the hope
that future generations will revere and bless them.
But the sage works so that future generations
will be free to follow their own paths
and live their own lives.

If we begrudge the younger generation
its enthusiasms or its dreams
it will only make us miserable.
Let us instead encourage their dreams,
support them with our wisdom,
and bless them with our prayers.
It is only fitting that the young inherit the world.
So did we.

Give freely of your leadership,
but don't worry about being appreciated.
Happily pass what wisdom you have gained
on to younger generations,
but don't worry about being valued.
Let them look ahead,
not behind.
We are their foundation,
they will supply the house.

18

REMEMBER WHO YOU ARE

Forgetting the Tao
brings bitter aging.
We demand proper behavior
and mourn its demise.
We look for faults
and always find them.
We criticize government
and withhold our own leadership.
We stop living at peace
with our family and friends,
and remember with longing
the good old days.

Remembering the Tao
brings joyous aging.
We become an encouraging presence for all.
We replace cynicism and complaint
with a satin sheen of compassion.

Never forget that your true nature
is that of a sage.
It is as effortless for you as breathing.
Pause a moment,
and remember who you are.

19

GOODNESS, LOVE, AND JOY

There are three advantages to growing older.
We no longer worry about becoming holy,
therefore we accept ourselves as we are.
We no longer worry about public opinion,
therefore we do what seems right within our own
       hearts.
We no longer worry about loss,
therefore we are content with whatever happens.
Goodness, love, and joy
have always been within us,
waiting to be noticed.

I look back on my life
and I wonder why I tried so hard
to be good,
to be loved,
and to be happy.
What wasted effort!

20

AN INFANT AT HER MOTHER'S BREAST

Becoming a sage is like becoming an infant
once more at her mother's breast,
peaceful and disturbed by no great worries.
It is like becoming homeless and wandering,
yet always at home wherever we are.
We are no longer excited
at every little change of fortune.
Our minds are no longer filled with details
and have more room for spaces of silence.
Lofty goals and grand purposes have faded,
replaced by a willingness to drift
wherever the Divine current takes us.

It is all right to loosen your hold on things.
To care less about some things,
and more about others.
You don't have to cling to your images of yourself.
Why try to take a thirty-year-old's mind
into your wisdom years?
Life *is* different now,
and wonderful!

Like the Full Moon on an Autumn Evening

When we were young
and feeling the need to prove ourselves,
we generated heat and energy
like the noonday sun.
But now we take time to reflect the Tao
and bathe our world in soft silent beauty
like the full moon on an Autumn evening.

An abundance of opinions will generate heat
but accomplish nothing.
You no longer have to comment
on each and every little thing.
You can observe events with a detached serenity.
When you speak,
your words are gentle, helpful, and few.
Your silence is as beautiful as the Harvest moon.

22

IF NOT YOU, WHO?

A youth may have ambitious goals
but the sage has no need for ambition.
A youth strives for perfection
but the sage is content with imperfection.
A youth is always on guard against loss
but the sage has let go already.

Therefore, despite the apparent advantages of youth,
it is the sage who shows the way.
It is the sage who can be trusted.
It is the sage who is the example to follow.
It is the sage who has succeeded.

You cannot fulfill your destiny
by hanging on to the qualities of youth.
If you do not display an alternative to blind
        ambition,
our world will be depleted beyond recovery.
If you do not live with acceptance and grace,
our world will be consumed by the fires of hate.
If you do not become a sage,
from where will guidance come?
If not you,
who?

23

Crack Yourself Open

Being a sage is not all unruffled calm.
It is also a time of freedom
to express and feel
the truth of our lives.
To explore the passions
buried for years
beneath acceptable masks.
It is time to serve a cause
with energy and compassion,
to fall madly in love
and dance into the night.

Crack yourself open!
What use is it to continue to hide
behind your facades and roles?
Why waste your energy playing games?
Isn't it time to cry your tears;
to shout your passion;
to dance like Zorba;
and to let your soul touch
the Soul of the world?

24

WAITING FOR THE POWER OF YOUR LOVE

Our hearts have always longed to love,
but have never been free of fear.
So we have always put aside
our natural compassion
and bowed before productivity
and security
and safety.

But now our vision is clearing,
our fears are lifting,
and we are beginning to see everything
through the eyes of love.

The same Soul that enlivened Mother Teresa
enlivens you.
Do you truly want to spend your golden years
in ever-increasing fear
and isolation?
Don't you secretly dream
of giving your life away
in pure unselfish love?
There are people waiting,
next door and around the globe,
waiting for the power of your love.

25

WE ARE A RIVER

Our life has not been an ascent
up one side of a mountain and down the other.
We did not reach a peak,
only to decline and die.
We have been as drops of water,
born in the ocean and sprinkled on the earth
in a gentle rain.
We became a spring,
and then a stream,
and finally a river flowing deeper and stronger,
nourishing all it touches
as it nears its home once again.

Don't accept the modern myths of aging.
You are not declining.
You are not fading away into uselessness.
You are a sage,
a river at its deepest
and most nourishing.
Sit by a riverbank sometime
and watch attentively as the river
tells you of your life.

26

Our Sleep Is Not as Deep

We are traveling more lightly now,
and our sleep is not as deep
as in our youth.
Restless thoughts stir the curtains
by the window of our mind.

It brings a blessed gift
of extra time set aside for the contemplation
we've been desiring.
A time for reading a book of quiet inspiration
or whispering a phrase of blessing
in rhythm with our breathing.
All the sleep we need
will be given us.

Don't be bothered by the restlessness.
Your soul is waking up
and naturally disturbs your mind.
Softly fold back the covers
and tiptoe to a quiet place
and sit contentedly
listening to your soul.

27

Why Would I Want to Go Back to Youth?

Nothing ever ends,
but something else begins.
The sage sees all events as disciplines
for refining the spirit.
As the outer vision develops difficulties,
the inner eye begins to see.
As muscles loose their youthful hardness,
flexibility and grace increase.
As the power of rank and position fades,
the energy of compassion and judgment rises.

I used to run marathons
and compete in triathalons.
Now I jog just a few miles a week,
but take long walks hand in hand
through the park
with my spouse.
My thoughts float on the Summer breeze
and my heart is filled with creative passion.
Why would I want to go back to youth?

28

WE HAVE BECOME THE LAMP

Once we grasped the things we needed
in closed and anxious fists.
Now our arms have opened wide
and the whole world has tumbled
into our lap.

Instead of looking to the world for answers
we have now become the answer.
Inside of us is all we ever needed,
and it is beginning to shine through.
Others can see it in our eyes.
We have become the very lamp
by which our path is illumined.

If you continue to conquer outer worlds,
who will take the journey inward
and discover the waiting treasure?
Who will light your path?

29

THE WISDOM TO
KNOW THE DIFFERENCE

The sage no longer strives
to make the world a better place,
thus it becomes better and better;
no longer worries about self-improvement,
thus improves daily;
no longer seeks to control other people,
thus receives love and trust from all;
no longer tampers with things,
thus sees all things unfold as they should
to take their place in the natural order of life.

Don't mistake the sage's serenity
for passivity.
We have not given up on important issues.
We now no longer attempt to change
that which cannot be changed.
We no longer ignore
that which can be changed.
And we finally have the wisdom
to know the difference.

30

THE SAGE MUST TRAVEL LIGHT

Youth can carry a heavy load day after day
without noticing the damaging effects.
But the sage must lay down the burden.
Resentments, regrets,
injuries, slights,
grudges, and disappointments
are much too cumbersome
for a person of wisdom and contentment.
The sage must travel light.

There is a backpack in the mind
which over the years has become
filled with rocks and stones.
You do not have to carry them anymore.
You can empty your pack
and carry only compassion
from one day to the next.

31

THE SAGE NO LONGER
GOES TO WAR

The sage no longer goes to war.
Athletics are for play and fun
instead of winning or losing.
Sexuality is for ecstasy and love
rather than conquest and self-indulgence.
Economics are for peace and justice
rather than mindless accumulation.
Relationships are vehicles for compassion
rather than struggles between egos.

Be alert for signs of continuing conflict within:
an angry voice, a tightening of the chest,
or a critical feeling.
Take a deep breath and disengage.
It is time to live
and to teach
a way of peace.

32

It Is Time to Focus

Do not be misled by myths
about the fading of the mind.
Meditation is the sage's lifeblood
and it can keep the mind fresh and pure,
capable of more beauty
than youth can imagine.

Much of the mind's activity
is merely automatic response
to external and internal stimuli;
endless chatter concerning
hunger, fear, desire, and distraction.
It is time to focus.
Only a focused mind
is capable of actual contemplative thought.
And the mind that contemplates
produces attitudes and actions
of compassion, peace, and beauty.

There are dozens of approaches to meditation.
Explore them.
Choose those that seem to fit you
and practice them every day.
This is as essential for the mind
as is food for the body!

33

GIFTS OF GREATEST BEAUTY

We have embraced those things which others
    shun.
Embracing death,
we find life.
Embracing uncertainty,
we find awe.
Embracing limitations,
we find the path of effective action.

Life is sweetest
only when we know that we will die.
Breathtaking wonder comes
only in the presence of indescribable mystery.
Correct actions emerge
only when we understand
what we can and cannot do.

The things you have feared the most
will be your greatest friends.
When they knock on your door,
welcome them with graciousness.
They seem unattractive
but they bear gifts of greatest beauty.

34

FREE TO BE EFFECTIVE

Our effectiveness increases as we age.
We are free of the millstone of reputation
and enjoy the blessings
of anonymity and humility
rather than the curses
of fame and pride.

We are like the Tao
which has hidden itself
within all things.
It is completely humble
but it alone endures.

It is time to cease worrying
about how you are perceived.
Not attracting attention to yourself,
you are free to be effective.
It is time to work behind the scenes,
in quiet and subtle ways.
It is time to make your greatest contribution
to your family and your world.

35

Hope Is Always Waiting

The sage sees life in deeper ways:
sees intricate patterns of beauty
embedded in life's fabric;
sees comfort woven within the pain;
sees gain shining amidst the loss;
sees forgiveness binding up resentment's wounds;
and sees life always rising out of death.

So much of our perception
is conditioned by our fears and our desires.
We must learn to see the things
that others cannot see.
Then we must assure them
of the beauty hidden there.

Look deeply into your life.
Search out the hidden things
within your present circumstances.
The beauty is there.
Comfort and forgiveness are available.
Hope is always waiting
for you to find.

36

READY TO RECEIVE

Fear of aging has its roots
in a fear of losing possessions, friends,
and control of life.
It might be wise to give these things away
and so no longer worry about their loss.

Having few possessions means freedom
from worry and fret.
Not clinging to friends means freedom
to enjoy them completely.
Not trying to control life means freedom
to be guided by the Tao.

There is loss in growing older.
But if you can manage not to cling
your hands will remain open,
ready to receive new gifts
of contentment, wisdom, and depth of soul.

37

Forever Limitless

The young confuse passion with desire,
and live in constant discontent.
The sage knows the difference
and lives in peace and joy.
Desiring nothing,
yet passionate about everything;
possessing nothing,
yet enjoying all;
the sage lives life to its fullest.

Our desires will never be completely satisfied,
but our passion for living will be its own
	satisfaction.
Desires, no matter how important they seem,
constrict and limit our life.
Passion, with all its pain and joy,
is forever limitless.

38

SINK DEEP

The sage is not disturbed
by the ripples and waves
that so disturb other people.
There is no need for hurry.
How others behave is of no great concern.
For in the deep waters
of the sage's world
there is always enough time,
always enough goodness,
and always enough love.

Younger people are often afraid to dive deep
so they remain tossed by the waves.
But you can learn to see beneath the surface of
        behavior,
and live in the deeper waters
where it is always cool and still.
The next time the behavior of others,
close at home or across the world,
disturbs you,
sink deep into the waters of your life.
There you will find all you need.

39

All the Beauty of the World Is Yours

One who has seen wildflowers
effortlessly blanket fields
each year for decades
does not become overly anxious
about what to eat or drink.
One who has for years
watched the Maple tree
release its leaves each Autumn,
and regain them every Spring,
has no great fear of loss.
One who has seen a thousand sunsets,
each unique and unrepeatable,
has little interest in society's attempts
to package, price, and sell
baubles it calls beautiful.

Don't believe the propaganda
of smiling gray-haired consumers
continuing the insane attempt
to spend their way to happiness.
You have become a sage
and you live at peace with all of nature.
All the beauty of the world is yours.

40

READY TO DEPART
AND TO ARRIVE

The world wants life without death
and arrival without departure.
The sage knows this is foolishness
and is always ready to depart
and to arrive.

The things that used to define you
are no longer adequate to do so.
There is no need to cling to them.
The closets of your mind can be cleaned
of ideas no longer needed.
When the time to depart is at hand,
you will be ready.
When something new arrives,
you will have room.

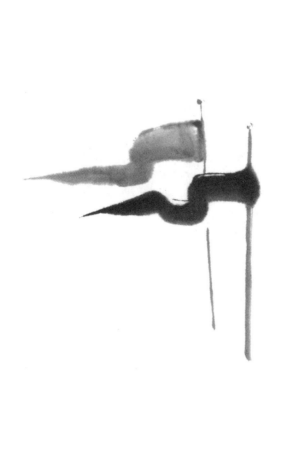

41

LIKE COMING HOME

One person embraces the flow of time,
and lets the passing years bring new wisdom.
This person becomes a sage.
Another person sometimes follows the unfolding
 path,
but keeps drawing back into familiar habits.
This person struggles all of life.
A third person rejects the path of wisdom
 altogether
and clings tenaciously to youth,
ridiculing the aged and vowing never to get "old."
Bitterness lurks just around the corner.

Learning to see things from a different angle
requires great courage.
Old voices within
will seek to kindle the fire of fear:
"You're not going to have enough.
You must hold on!
You're going to be alone.
You're going to die."

This is the truth of the Tao:
We will always have enough.
We can let go.
We are never alone.
And dying will be like coming home.

42

A Weaving Made of Love

The time is coming
when all the scattered parts of life
will blend in a harmonious whole.
The high points and the triumphs,
the sins and the failures,
the bravery and the cowardliness,
the youthful aspirations and the adult regrets
will become strands in one single weaving
that will reveal itself as made of love.

You do not have to brace yourself
against your fears of future shocks.
Such bracing stiffens your joints
and stirs your thoughts.
You can welcome the future
as you welcome a lover,
with openness, trust, and joy.

43

AGENTS OF GRACE

The sage can find a welcome
in the most inhospitable places
because no one perceives a threat.
People soften in the sage's presence
and minds open up to learning.
Kindly spoken words
open doors that crowbars couldn't budge.

We can transform family gatherings
not by our demands but by our smiles.
We can enliven conversations
rather than dominate them.
We are becoming agents of grace and hope,
rather than of tyranny and despair.

44

SUCCESS IS AN INSIDE JOB

Youth strives for outer signs
that demonstrate success.
The sage sees success
as an inside job
and has learned to value attitudes
rather than symbols.
Cultivating peace and compassion within,
the sage no longer needs to search
high and low, near and far,
for temporary trinkets.

If today you seek
to increase your net financial worth,
you may or may not succeed.
If today you seek
to increase your serenity and wisdom,
I guarantee you will succeed.

45

PERFECTION WILL BE BUILT

Trying to make a perfect life
is a path of great sorrow.
The perfect life cannot be built
by seeking to fulfill desires
no matter how many years are spent,
or how much effort is applied.
Desires are insatiable and endless.

If instead we see
the imperfect events,
and the ordinary people,
as the movement of the Tao,
life becomes perfect as it is.

The time comes when we realize
that the ducks will never be in a row.
It is the nature of ducks to fly about.
The house will never be perfectly clean.
It is the nature of a house to accommodate clutter.
The project will never be done just right.
It is the nature of projects to evolve into other
        projects.
The future will never be perfectly secure.
It is the nature of life to be unpredictable.

Sit still and watch for a moment.
Perfection will be built
from all that is imperfect.

46

WHAT IS BEING NURTURED WITHIN ME?

Words and images are designed
to stimulate fears, desires, and prejudices.
Fears increase and breed violence.
Desires increase and breed dissatisfaction.
Prejudices are reinforced and breed fear.
The circle continues.

So the sage reads with great care,
views with discernment,
and listens with mindfulness.

We fret about the viewing habits
of the younger generation
and rate their movies G or R.
But we have habits formed by years
of exposure to the media.
Each book, program, and newspaper
must be approached with subtle awareness.
Do I read and watch for wisdom,
or to torture my fears
and reinforce my prejudices?
What is being nurtured within me?

47

It Is Never Too Late

It is never too late to become a sage,
never too early to begin.
There is no seminar to attend,
no certification to obtain.
There is no quest to undertake,
no mountain to climb.
We simply wake up,
and look around,
and understand.

Where are you at this moment?
Can you sit quietly for a bit,
and look about?
Lay aside your wants and fears,
desires and hopes,
for just a minute.
Can you feel the Sage inside?

48

What Will Be Left
Is Life Itself

Each day that passes,
the sage discards another useless weight.
Finally all the accumulated burden
of a life spent seeking something
is gone.
In its place is a lightness of being
and a clarity of seeing
that makes a heaven
of each moment.

Make it your daily discipline
to lay aside one little thing;
a tiny fear, a simple preconception,
a useless book, a piece of household clutter,
a habit of avoidance, a bit of shame or guilt,
a desire that distracts,
even a good intention.
What will be left is Life Itself.

49

SEE THE WORLD AS A BETTER PLACE

The sage brings justice to the world
by seeing beyond justice.

No longer needing to balance the scales,
the sage can now remove the scales
that block clear vision.

The sage sees all beings as innocent,
and all people as beloved.
This allows justice to flow.

If you truly want to leave the world a better place,
you must release your need to do so.
Dedicate your remaining years
to seeing the world as a better place,
rather than making it better.
When you see it so,
you begin to make it so.

50

Without Resistance

Resistance is the opponent of the sage.
Resistance in the mind
allows no new thinking.
Resistance of the body
brings stiffness and disease.
Resistance of the spirit
makes a sorrow of life and death.

Without resistance
the sage welcomes life
and death as one.
Without resistance
action and rest flow together
and life becomes full of joy.

Resisting our aging process
brings about the very pain
we fear.
Let the flexibility and grace of Yoga
replace power lifting at the gym.
Let the grace of new ideas
be welcomed in our minds each day.
Both life and death will become our friends.

51

WE ARE BECOMING
EMBRACERS OF LIFE

The sage accomplishes much
by expecting nothing particular.
People are just people,
events are just events,
life is just life,
and death is just death.
The sage embraces
people, events, life, and death
unconditionally.

This the sage learned from the Tao,
which enfolds all things
in an unconditional embrace of love.

We are not becoming optimistic,
nor pessimistic,
nor stoic.
We are becoming embracers of life.

52

IT IS A MATTER OF CHOICE

The world has said
that those who do the right things,
choose the right careers,
work hard,
and avoid mistakes,
shall satisfy their desires
and be at peace.

The sage knows
that this is an illusion born of fear.
Great accomplishments do not bring peace.
Massive failures do not bring despair.
The choice between peace
and despair
is an inner choice
that may be made at any moment.

I see much despair among the aging
that is so unnecessary.
Our history does not determine our present.
Peace is always available to us.
It is a matter of choice.

53

True Rewards of Aging

Do not succumb to the lie
that the second half of life
should be a time of increasing luxury and ease.
Baubles galore are offered to older persons
as seeming rewards for all their work.
Their increasing years are accompanied
by increasing pressures to consume.

The sage sees these trinkets as symbols
of foolishness, not of power.
The luxury of a serene mind and spirit
is preferred to that of leather seats.
The pleasure of compassion
is preferred to that of isolation.

Is comfort and luxury
really what it has all been about?
Rich or poor,
we must adjust our thinking.
Serenity and compassion are the true rewards of
aging.
Anything else is superfluous.

54

EMBRACING THE TAO IS ENOUGH

Embracing the Tao,
we do not fear fading away.
The more we age,
the brighter we become.
We become humble,
and find we are honored.
We stop meddling in the lives of others,
and find that our influence increases.
We forget about ourselves,
and are remembered by all.

This paradox cannot be evaded.
"Perhaps by learning humility,
I will become a person of fame."
Not a chance.
Power and fame are meaningless.
Embracing the Tao is enough.

55

DISAPPOINTMENTS DISAPPEAR

A newborn child has no complicated desires.
It knows nothing of sexuality,
yet its genitals bring it pleasure.
It cries when hungry and sleeps when tired.
It therefore knows great harmony.
But time brings complicated desires,
which lead to disappointments,
and disappointments age the mind and body.

The sage returns to infancy.
Desires become simple
so disappointments disappear.
Pleasure becomes intense
and harmony returns.

Certain attitudes age us more than others.
Sadness and grief are natural
and heal quite readily.
But always wishing things
had worked out differently
withers our spirit
and makes us older than we are.

56

THE POWER
IN OUR LATER LIFE

Great displays of power
reveal an underlying impotence.
But the sage has subtle power:
the power of silent listening;
the power of friendly eyes;
the power of a gentle smile;
the power of a serene spirit.
This power is anchored
in the potency of the Tao.
Nothing can withstand it.

How refreshing not to have to strut about
like a Bantam rooster in a coop.
We have nothing to prove anymore.
Disgrace and honor mean the same to us—
nothing!
Our power in our later life
will give birth to many wonders.

57

A Lasting Legacy

If you want a lasting legacy,
show how to be secure
without being wealthy;
show how to be safe
without owning an arsenal;
show how to be spiritual
without being religious;
show how to be serene
without controlling events;
and show how to die
without being disturbed.

There are very few
who can pass on such a legacy.
I knew one such.
That was enough to change my life.
Are you spending your efforts
on the right sort of estate?

58

TREAT YOURSELF AS A GRANDCHILD

Nurture yourself as you age
as you would nurture a newborn infant.
Scolding yourself will break your spirit.
Pushing yourself will damage your health.
Laughing and playing will strengthen your immune
    system.
Forgiving yourself completely will make your heart
    strong.
Hugging and cuddling will heal your wounds.

I know too many grandparents
who dote on their grandchildren,
yet punish themselves for not living up to
impossible standards.
Remember that you, too,
are a beloved child of the Tao.

59

How Happy We All Become

What freedom there is
in needing no achievement.
No longer struggling with life,
the sage uses anything life brings
for good.
Because nothing particular is needed,
nothing is impossible.
Universal compassion
is as natural as breathing.

We are at last able
to move amidst our loved ones
with the grace of a dancer.
And they are at last free
of our clumsy attempts to control.
How happy we all become.

60

SAVE TIME FOR THE TAO

The sage does not get bothered
by the daily concerns of life;
does not fret and fuss and poke around,
always stirring the pot of anxiety.
Work gets done and decisions are made,
but the sage has stepped aside.
The tasks handle themselves.

You don't have to withdraw
and hope your concerns will go away.
But neither do you have to invest them
with the energy of worry.
Do what is necessary, no more.
Save some time for exploring the Tao
in all its mystery and wonder.

61

THERE IS ALWAYS SOMETHING MORE TO LEARN

Age brings a gentle humility to life.
No longer defensive and afraid,
we can move easily through the day.
Mistakes no longer immobilize us
but merely deepen our wisdom
with the hopeful message,
"There is always something more to learn."

The mind of the expert is narrowly trained.
The mind of the sage is opening wide.
We are not becoming experts.
We are just finally becoming good students.

There are so many wonders yet to see.
Don't waste today
on reinforcing your views and opinions.
Learn something wholly new
about your spouse,
your child,
your friend,
your world.

62

Open to All

To become a sage
it is not necessary to have lived
a good and pious life.
The way of the sage is open to all,
good and bad,
clever and simple,
leader and follower.
Why?
Because the Tao welcomes all,
forgives all,
and teaches its lessons
to any who will listen.

Nothing you have done
or not done
can block your way.
Don't make your future depend
on your biased review of your past.
A life of wisdom is open to us all
always.

63

ATTENTION TO DETAIL

Attention to detail
comes with growing older.
Things that once were done unconsciously
now take conscious effort.
This is a wondrous benefit.
A slower walking pace reveals songbirds
never seen before.
A slower working pace reveals opportunities
never explored before.
A slower living pace reveals beauty
never experienced before.

We are slowing down,
but waking up.
We are producing less,
but learning more.
We are doing less,
and experiencing more.

64

ANOTHER WAY

No grand visions of holiness,
just a simple placing
of one foot in front of the other
leads us along the path.

Having nothing more to gain,
nothing left to finish,
leaves us calm
and able to see without fear.
Therefore we bring
clarity to confusion,
and comfort to suffering.

Healing of this world's painful wounds
is now your task,
and the healing of your own
is the first step.
It is time to lay aside the ambition
that has perpetuated wounding,
and let your growing contentment
speak of another way.

65

When a Flower Was a Flower

Philosophers grapple with questions
of the meaning and purpose of life.
Theologians engage in endless debates
over the nature and aspects of God.
Biologists dissect and probe
beneath the surface of all living things.
But the sage just looks at the Tao
as it dances through all of life,
and smiles and enjoys
his ignorance.

When we first began to learn,
things became more and more complex.
Now things become simpler and simpler.
We are returning to the direct apprehension of life
that we had when we were children,
when a flower was a flower
and we laughed and cried with ease.

66

It Is Time to Really Live

The youth stands outside of life
and wonders about it.
The adult engages life
and wrestles with it.
The sage, with arms open wide,
lets life flow through,
like a river on its way to the sea.

Cast away the worries
that so limited your earlier years.
Welcome each dawn
with expectation and glee.
Let the day flow into you,
and out of you,
in contentment and joy.
It is time to really live.

67

ALLOWING PEACE AT LAST

Instead of a jumble of scattered thoughts,
our minds now have a simple clarity,
seeing directly into pain and pleasure.
Instead of anxious fretful worry,
we now experience a patience of body and soul,
welcoming people as they are.
Instead of judgment and complaint,
we now bring a compassionate embrace of self and
    others,
allowing peace at last.

Stop for a moment and let your thoughts
gradually wind down.
How long does it take
before there is a restful emptiness?
How long can you remain there,
unruffled and still?
This is your training ground.
Here you are becoming a sage.

68

Dancing in the Winds of Change

The child rightly expects
to be cared for by others.
The youth still expects this,
but rebels against it
and lives in confusion and turmoil.
The adult works hard at arranging externals
in an attempt to provide security,
and lives in constant fear of losing everything.

But the sage plays life as a grand game,
seeing hard times as honorable opponents,
increasing wisdom and refining skill.

Your financial or physical status is irrelevant
to your progress as a sage.
You may make decisions that do not work
as you had expected.
You may lose rather than gain security.
It does not matter.
Your mission is to become a sage.
A calm and supple person,
dancing in the winds of change.

69

ACHIEVING ALL

The sage is active but not combative.
Obstacles are no longer enemies
and do not yield to attack.
Instead the sage sits with a clear mind
and observes the obstacle mindfully
until it is completely understood.
Understood,
it disappears.

When I was young,
achieving my goal was more important
than understanding the situation.
Therefore my achievements were few and partial.
Now I look first for understanding.
Achieving that,
I achieve all.

70

No Need to Be Understood

Adults and youth often see the sage
as just an older man or woman.
They don't see the quietness behind the eyes
nor the serenity behind the smile.
They can't sense the power of the soul
nor the strength of the spirit.
But the sage understands so deeply
that there is no need to be understood.

I often find myself dismissed
by the younger, driven folk,
as that quiet older gentleman
who sits and drinks his coffee as he writes
at the corner table by the window.
That is fine by me.

71

DANCING WITH THE TAO

How can we tell when we become sages?
We cannot tell.
We can only see our actions and attitudes
that are still born of fear and foolishness,
and recognize them for what they are.
Those actions and attitudes born of wisdom
flow so effortlessly they are not noticed.
All we are aware of is increasing clarity and serenity.

When I am off-balance I react
with fear, anger, and confusion.
When I am more balanced I react
with awareness and effectiveness.
When I am completely balanced in my soul,
I am not aware of acting at all.
I am dancing with the Tao.

72

ON THE PATH AGAIN

The sage is a signpost
pointing the way to wisdom and peace.
If people say, "how wise
and wonderful you are,"
the sage flees the scene
lest people become enamored with the signpost
and lose sight of the path itself.

When I am aware of my need
to be seen and to be respected,
I know that I am lost.
(And I am often lost.)
When I see only the other person
with clarity and compassion,
we are both on the path again.

73

Fearless out of Wisdom

The youth is fearless
out of foolishness.
The sage is fearless
out of wisdom.
The youth feels invulnerable
and acts without awareness.
The sage knows vulnerability
and acts with mindful care.
The youth has strength
but does not know the Tao.
The sage seems weak
but accesses the power of All Things.

Discovering my strengths has been a benefit.
But discovering my true weaknesses
and acknowledging them to myself
has been my power growing older.
I see myself for who I am.
No illusions.
Great serenity.

74

WATCH IT COME AND GO

Looking back on life we see
that nothing remained the same.
Things came
and went
without our permission or control.
The future will unfold in the same manner.
What is there to do
but sit in mindful appreciation
and watch it come
and go.

Work with passion and energy
at the tasks you cherish,
but connect often with that part of you
that is watching it all happen
with eternal joy and love.

75

JOY AND SORROW
BECOME ONE

Watching people scramble
in pursuit of wealth and pleasure,
we long to tell them what we've learned
of the simple things of life.
Watching people beg for food
along our city streets,
we long to bring them hope.
Seeing rich and poor as one,
we live as does the Tao,
loving all without discrimination.

Opening your heart to all
is a painful process
because it makes you feel so helpless.
This helpless feeling is the beginning of
compassion.
Live with it until your heart melts
and you enter that place
where distinctions disappear
and joy and sorrow become one.

76

The Light Within the Darkness

As the body weakens, the spirit grows stronger.
As the joints stiffen, the mind grows more flexible.
As the heart grows tired, the courage awakens.
As the steps wobble, the soul remains unmoved.
The radiance of the sage becomes
the light within the darkness of the world.

Can you imagine millions
of strong-spirited,
free-thinking,
courageous elders
living in our cities and towns?
It is my hope for the world.

77

BALANCE

The sage has achieved life's balance.
Work gives way to rest,
and returns again to work
without resistance.
Health gives way to illness
and returns again to health
without worry.
Life gives way to death
and returns again to life
without fear.

Let the yin and yang of life
do their dance in perfect harmony.
Everything has its place and time.
The coming and the going
is not a problem.
It is not stability that you need,
it is balance.

Your Time of Greatest Power

Our lives have become fluid as water
and as flexible as a young plant.
Instead of the "hard body" of gym commercials,
we have bodies of grace and gentleness.
Instead of rigid attitudes of self-righteousness,
we have minds of open trust.
Instead of breaking in the storms of life,
we have bent and sprung back.
Nothing can cause us despair
for we are one with the Tao.

You are not diminishing.
Each day that passes brings you deeper strength.
Your serenity increases each moment.
Your dying breath will be
your time of greatest power.

FAILURE IS THE FAITHFUL COMPANION

Failure is the faithful companion of the sage.
No other mentor is as wise or true.
But this companionship is a difficult one,
and requires great attention and skill.
The lessons must be learned without rancor or
      depression;
without bitterness or blame of others.
Mistakes must not be hidden or repressed
but welcomed as beloved friends.
Arrogant and fearful people glory in their
      achievements.
The wise and content cherish their mistakes.

The ability to review our lives
without regret or shame
is not the reward of the blameless,
for such do not exist.
It is the reward of the courageous
who accept each failure
as a stepping stone to wisdom.
When you can review the hidden portions of your
      life
with peace and acceptance,
you will be a sage.

80

What Other Reason Could There Be?

Life is always too short.
We will never be able to see
everything we wanted to see,
do all the things we wanted to do,
or achieve all the successes
we thought so important.
But to arrive at a quiet mind,
and a serene spirit,
is the supreme accomplishment.
If we do this,
we have done all.

Do what you can each day.
Enjoy your goals and plans.
But the cultivation of your spirit
is your greatest task.
What other reason could there be
for the life you have been given?

81

THE TRUTH OF GROWING OLDER

The truth of growing older
cannot be described,
only experienced.

We are unaware of becoming sages,
we just know that we are at peace.
We are unaware of being wise,
we just know that we are content.
We are unaware of being generous,
we just enjoy giving ourselves away.

May your coming years be filled
with all the blessings of the sage.
May you live your years with peace and joy.
May you die content and happy,
knowing all is well;
that it has always been so
and will always be so.

ACKNOWLEDGMENTS

■

I AM GRATEFUL for the encouragement and guidance of my dear colleagues, friends, and family—all of whom embody the Tao in my life:

Matthew Lore, my editor at The Experiment, whose spirit and skill have supported and refined my work.

Barbara Moulton, my agent, who has patiently endured my many moments of non-Tao–like fretting and fuming, kept me on track, and returned me to center.

Hank Tusinski, whose illustrations have once again captured the spirit of the Tao in simple, elegant brush strokes.

Chungliang Huang, for his continuing encouragement and for his lovely foreword to this volume.

My children, Lara and John, who love their dad regardless.

My dear spouse, Nancy, who loves me and sees the sage within me.

To all of you my deepest thanks.

■

WILLIAM MARTIN, husband and father of two grown children, has been a student of the Tao for twenty-five years, and is the author of numerous other Tao-inspired books, including *The Parent's Tao Te Ching*. A graduate of the University of California, Berkeley, and Western Theological Seminary, he has worked as a research scientist for the Department of the Navy, a clergyman, and a college instructor in counseling, communications, and the humanities. Today, he and his wife Nancy operate The Still Point, a center for Taoist/Zen practice, where he conducts workshops and seminars on the application of Taoist and Zen thought to the issues of everyday life. They live in Chico, California. William Martin can be reached by e-mail at bill@thestillpoint.com.